THE SECOND WORLD WAR FOR CHILDREN

IN PARTNERSHIP WITH

IWM
IMPERIAL WAR MUSEUMS

PETER CHRISP

CARLTON KiDS

SECOND WORLD WAR
ACROSS THE WORLD

This is a map of the world in September 1942. It shows Allied and Axis countries, and territory under their control or influence. Major battles of the Second World War are also indicated.

MAP KEY

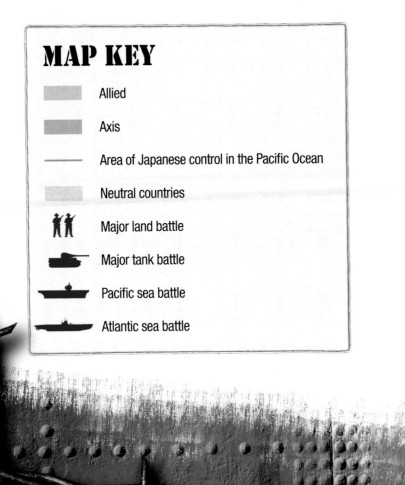

Allied

Axis

Area of Japanese control in the Pacific Ocean

Neutral countries

Major land battle

Major tank battle

Pacific sea battle

Atlantic sea battle

GREENLAND

ICELAND

CANADA

Ottawa

Washington, DC • New York

UNITED STATES OF AMERICA (USA)

BATTLE OF THE ATLANTIC

IRELAND BR Lo

D-DAY

SPA

PORTUGAL

ATLANTIC OCEAN

West Indies

Dakar •

FREN A

VENEZUELA

COLOMBIA

ECUADOR

PERU

BRAZIL

BOLIVIA

CHILE ARGENTINA

A WORLD AT WAR

The Second World War, from 1939–45, was the biggest and deadliest conflict in history. Many countries took part and fighting took place all around the world. More than 55 million people were killed, most of them civilians.

Unlike previous wars, which were mainly fought between armies on battlefields, the Second World War was a "people's war". Civilians were at the centre of the action, as cities were devastated by aerial bombing. Workers on the "home front", making armaments and growing food, were as important to victory in the war as soldiers.

RIGHT: German and Italian tanks at El Alamein, in the North African desert.

ABOVE: A Japanese cruiser in flames during the 1942 Battle of Midway, in the middle of the Pacific.

LEFT: Finnish ski troops fighting in the winter snow against the Soviets.

IN EVERY CLIMATE

The war was fought on land, at sea, in the air and in every possible climate and landscape. Soldiers battled in the steamy jungle of South East Asia and in the winter snow of Russia. Great tank armies rolled through the North African desert. Across the wide Pacific Ocean there were sea battles between the biggest naval forces in history. Beneath the Atlantic, German submarines, called U-boats, hunted convoys of merchant ships. Sea battles were even fought in the Arctic, in winter when the sun does not rise above the horizon.

NEW WAYS OF FIGHTING

The war saw many new ways of fighting. Cities on each side were heavily bombed, in order to destroy people's will to fight. For the first time, invasions were carried out by air, by paratroopers. The development of the aircraft carrier – a warship that carries fighter aircraft – meant that air battles could be fought in the middle of the ocean. There were many new inventions, as scientists on each side raced to find war-winning weapons. These included jet-powered fighter planes and the German V-2 rocket – the first ballistic, or guided, missile. Most deadly of all was the atomic bomb, a single bomb powerful enough to destroy a whole city in seconds.

LEFT: German paratroopers land in Crete, Greece, in May 1941, taking part in the first aerial invasion – or invasion from the air.

> **"The whole of the warring nations are engaged, not only soldiers, but the entire population. . . The fronts are everywhere."**
>
> Winston Churchill, August 1940

ABOVE: The ruins of the city of Dresden, Germany, following two massive bombing raids in February 1945.

THE GATHERING STORM

BELOW: Hitler at the 1934 Nuremberg Rally, one of the huge party meetings that were staged to display Nazi power and unity.

There was a slow build up to the outbreak of the Second World War. The First World War, of 1914–18, left Europe in ruins, and up to 21 million dead. Afterwards, the victors redrew the map of Europe, punishing the losing nations, Germany and Austria.

Under the Treaty of Versailles, drawn up by Britain, France and the United States in 1919, the Austrian Empire was broken up, and several new countries created. Germany lost territory to Poland and France and had to give up its large army. Blamed for starting the war, the Germans also had to pay huge sums of money to the winning nations. Most Germans felt humiliated by the Treaty of Versailles. The treaty was opposed by a new political party called the National Socialist German Workers' Party, or Nazi Party. Its leader, from 1921, was Adolf Hitler, an ex-soldier with a domineering personality. Hitler believed that the German Army had not been defeated, but stabbed in the back by the traitors who agreed to the Treaty.

DENMARK
Baltic Sea
North Sea
Danzig
EAST PRUSSIA
Hamburg
Berlin
POLAND
Warsaw
NETHERLANDS
GERMANY
River Rhine
BELGIUM
Frankfurt
Prague
CZECHOSLOVAKIA
FRANCE
River Danube
Munich
AUSTRIA

GERMANY, 1919

Germany before 1919

Parts of Germany lost after the Treaty of Versailles

HITLER'S RISE TO POWER

In 1929, there was a worldwide financial crisis, which led to soaring unemployment. In Germany, the government appeared to be unable to deal with the crisis. People wanted strong leadership, which Hitler promised to provide. In the election of July 1932, the Nazis won the largest number of seats in the Reichstag, or Parliament. Hitler, appointed Chancellor (head of government) in January 1933, went on to ban the other political parties. He took on the title of Führer, meaning "leader". He was racist and held Jewish people widely responsible for Germany's misfortunes.

ABOVE: In New York, United States, women queue for food following the economic crisis of 1929, which left millions unemployed worldwide.

BELOW: The Nazi message was that, under Hitler, there was "One People, One Reich (realm), One Führer".

13. MÄRZ 1938
EIN VOLK EIN REICH.
EIN FÜHRER

NAZIS AND FASCISTS

The Nazis had much in common with the Italian Fascists, whose leader, Benito Mussolini, ruled Italy as a dictator, from 1922. Hitler and Mussolini presented themselves as saviours, who would restore national pride, and who demanded total obedience. Their parties were military in style, with uniforms and special symbols and salutes. Mussolini and Hitler were political allies prior to and during the Second World War.

RIGHT: Like Hitler, Mussolini was a powerful speaker, who inspired followers to be loyal and devoted to him.

STEPS TO WAR

After making himself dictator of Germany in 1933, Adolf Hitler was in a position to break the hated Treaty of Versailles. Hitler guessed, correctly, that the British and French would do little to stop him.

Hitler's first move was to build up Germany's armed forces. At first he did this in secret. It was only in 1935, after the Luftwaffe, or air force, had 2,500 planes, and the army had 300,000 soldiers, that he revealed that Germany was rearming. The following year, he sent troops into the Rhineland, a part of Germany that was supposed to be free of military forces. This was a threat to France, but even though France protested, it did not act. Then, in 1938, the German army marched into Austria, and the two German-speaking nations were united.

LEFT: The symbol of the Nazi party was the swastika – a cross with arms bent at right angles. Red, black and white were colours of the old German empire.

MUNICH CONFERENCE

After seizing Austria, Hitler threatened neighbouring Czechoslovakia. He demanded the Sudetenland, a Czech region with a population of over three million German speakers. In September 1938, Chamberlain and Daladier, the British and French leaders, held a conference with Mussolini and Hitler in Munich. They agreed to make Czechoslovakia surrender the Sudetenland. In return, Hitler promised that this was his final demand. Although Hitler had got his way, he was disappointed by the Munich Agreement. He had been looking forward to conquering the whole of Czechoslovakia, not just the Sudetenland.

BELOW: Nazi supporters pull down frontier signs between Germany and Czechoslovakia. With the German occupation, Czechoslovakia ceased to exist.

CZECHOSLOVAKIA, 1939
Czechoslovakia in 1937
Parts of Czechoslovakia occupied by Germany

APPEASEMENT

The British Prime Minister, Neville Chamberlain, felt that Germany had been unfairly treated by the Treaty of Versailles, and that some of Hitler's actions were justified. So he followed a policy called "appeasement" – giving in to Hitler's demands in the hope of avoiding war. Hitler repeatedly lied to Chamberlain, claiming that each of his demands was the final one.

BELOW: On his return from the Munich Conference, Neville Chamberlain shows the public his signed agreement with Hitler.

THREATS TO POLAND

In March 1939, Hitler broke the promise made at Munich, and took over the rest of Czechoslovakia. Next he began to threaten Poland, demanding the return of the city of Danzig and the "Polish corridor" dividing Germany and East Prussia. At last, Chamberlain and Daladier decided to resist him. They warned Hitler that, if he attacked Poland, they would declare war on Germany. However Hitler, who had seen them back down in the past, did not believe they really intended to fight.

ABOVE: A helmet belonging to a soldier in the German army.

BLITZKRIEG ON POLAND

On 1 September 1939, Adolf Hitler launched a surprise attack on Poland. Following bombing raids on Polish aerodromes, German tanks and armed vehicles swept over the borders, invading from the north, west and south.

The invasion saw a new type of warfare, called "Blitzkrieg", or "lightning war". Its main features were surprise, speed and a concentration of forces. To surprise the enemy, the Germans attacked without even declaring war on Poland. By attacking small sections of the Polish defences, they concentrated their forces, allowing them to break through, and then sweep behind, enemy lines. The Poles faced the task of defending a 2,800-km (1,750-mile) long border. They had a large army of 800,000 men, but it was old-fashioned, with 11 brigades of horse-mounted troops and only a few tanks.

LEFT: Polish cavalrymen fought bravely, but they had little chance against German tanks.

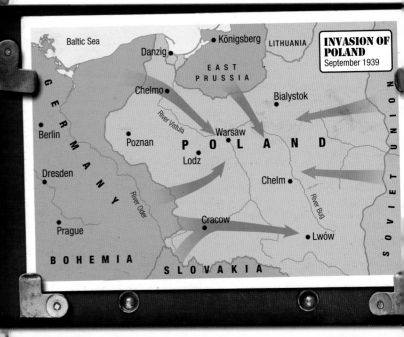

INVASION OF POLAND
September 1939

BELOW: By dive-bombing, a Stuka could hit targets, such as bridges or troop columns with great accuracy.

RIGHT: German tanks sweep across the Polish plains. In the dry summer of 1939, this was perfect terrain for tanks.

SHOCK WEAPONS

One aim of Blitzkrieg was to shock enemy troops, destroying their ability to fight back. The German Ju 87 Stuka dive-bomber, fitted with a screeching siren, was designed to cause terror as well as destruction. Armed with two machine guns and carrying five bombs, it plunged out of the sky at a steep angle, and at such speed that its pilots sometimes blacked out. An automatic brake allowed a Stuka to pull out of a dive even if its pilot had temporarily lost consciousness.

"Poland will never rise again in the form of the Versailles Treaty."

Adolf Hitler, 19 September 1939

THE WAR WIDENS

Two days after the invasion began, Britain and France honoured their guarantee to the Poles and declared war on Germany. Yet they could not protect Poland, and were stunned by the speed of the German invasion. The final blow came on 17 September, when the Soviet Union, or USSR, invaded Poland from the east. Joseph Stalin, the Soviet leader, had made a secret agreement with Hitler to divide Poland between them. He wanted to get his share before Hitler conquered the whole country.

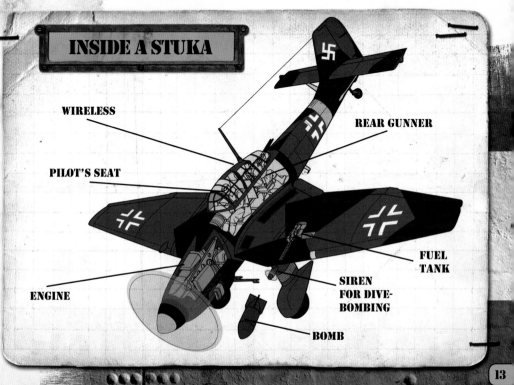

INSIDE A STUKA

WIRELESS

REAR GUNNER

PILOT'S SEAT

FUEL TANK

ENGINE

SIREN FOR DIVE-BOMBING

BOMB

HOME FRONT: BRITAIN

At the outbreak of war it was expected that British cities would be heavily bombed by the Germans. To meet the threat, the government organized Air Raid Precautions (ARP). Gas masks were handed out in case of gas attacks, cities were blacked out and children were evacuated to the country.

It was feared that in the event of bombing there would be a panic flight from the cities. The government decided to evacuate, or withdraw, young children and mothers with babies from threatened areas. In a huge operation, evacuees, accompanied by teachers, were sent by train to the countryside, where host families were found to take them in. This was a shock for the evacuees, most of whom had never seen the countryside. Their hosts were equally shocked at the newcomers, who sometimes came from very poor urban areas. When the expected air raids did not come, many parents took their children back to the cities.

RIGHT: The Government called on members of the public to serve as Air Raid Wardens. Around 1.5 million men and women volunteered for ARP duties.

Air Raid Wardens WANTED

ABOVE: A young girl evacuee, with her doll and luggage, waits nervously to be chosen by a host family.

ABOVE: An Air Raid Warden gives directions to a family wearing gas masks, during a practice drill for an air raid.

AIR RAID PRECAUTION WARDENS

It was the job of ARP wardens to enforce the "blackout". The blackout's purpose was to stop bomber planes finding cities at night. Street lights were put out, and people drew thick black curtains across their windows. Wardens patrolled the streets, shouting, "Put that light out!". In the event of a raid, sirens sounded the alarm and wardens guided people to shelters. They also distributed gas masks, and showed people how to put them on. The Germans were expected to drop bombs releasing poisonous gas.

RATIONING

Britain imported most of its food from overseas, using supply routes that became threatened by German submarines. To make sure everyone got a fair share, and to prevent people from hoarding food, on 8 January 1940 the government introduced rationing. Every person received a ration book, containing coupons to be handed to a shopkeeper when they bought goods. As well as food, petrol, coal and clothing were also rationed.

RIGHT: People were encouraged to grow carrots in their back gardens.

DOCTOR CARROT *the Children's best friend*

MINISTRY OF FOOD
RATION BOOK 1944-45
(GENERAL)
Surname HER MAJESTY
Other Names QUEEN MARY

RIGHT: The British Royal family was issued with ration books, to show that nobody had special privileges.

PURE · DRIED WHOLE **EGGS**

FRAY BENTOS SCOTCH BROTH

LEFT: Meat was in short supply. This tin of broth was brought across the Atlantic, from Uruguay.

LEFT: Powdered egg was widely used during the war.

⚔ WARTIME RECIPE

DIG FOR VICTORY!

"Dig for Victory" was a campaign to encourage people to grow food in their gardens to help the war effort. Recipes were provided by the government, to show people how to use the vegetables they grew. Here's a wartime recipe using potatoes instead of eggs (which were in short supply):

– EGG-LESS MAYONNAISE –

1 small potato mashed, 1 tsp mustard, 1 tsp vinegar, 125 ml vegetable oil, salt and pepper

Mash the potato until very smooth. Add the mustard and vinegar and mix well. Gradually add the oil, while stirring the mixture. Season with salt and pepper.

DIG FOR VICTORY

ABOVE: Millions of "Dig for Victory" posters and leaflets were distributed to the public.

WOMEN'S LAND ARMY

Over 80,000 women volunteered to become "Land Girls", members of the Women's Land Army, set up to replace male farm workers who had joined the armed forces. Wearing a uniform of brown breeches and green jerseys, they drove tractors, milked cows, dug potatoes and worked in sawmills.

BELOW: Members of the Women's Land Army preparing the soil to plant radishes.

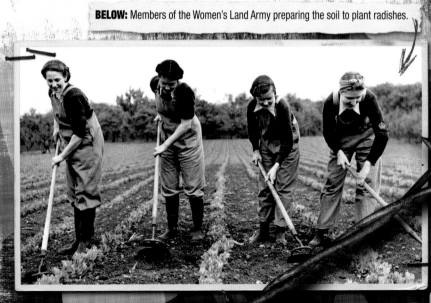

FALL OF FRANCE

Following the conquest of Poland, there was little fighting for several months. This period, nicknamed the "Phony War", ended when Germany invaded Norway and Denmark. Then, on 10 May 1940, Hitler launched a new Blitzkrieg against the Netherlands, Belgium and France.

The campaign began with an aerial attack on the Netherlands and northern Belgium, where 4,000 German paratroopers seized bridges and airfields. Motorized divisions then swept over the borders. The British and French advanced into Belgium to meet the invasion, not realizing that they had walked into a trap. For the main German forces were further south, where they broke through French lines in the Ardennes. This wooded region was wrongly thought to be unsuitable for tanks and was thinly defended. Once they had made the breakthrough, the German tanks raced north, towards the English Channel, encircling the British and French armies.

ABOVE: The Dutch surrendered after Rotterdam, their largest industrial city and port, was heavily bombed in May.

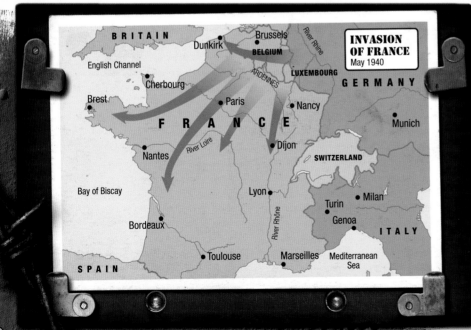

INVASION OF FRANCE
May 1940

BRITAIN
English Channel
Brussels
BELGIUM
Dunkirk
River Rhine
ARDENNES
LUXEMBOURG
GERMANY
Cherbourg
Brest
Paris
Nancy
Munich
FRANCE
River Loire
Nantes
Dijon
SWITZERLAND
Bay of Biscay
Lyon
River Rhône
Turin
Milan
Bordeaux
Genoa
ITALY
Toulouse
Marseilles
Mediterranean Sea
SPAIN

ABOVE: French infantrymen surrender to the Germans.

RETREAT TO DUNKIRK

Though the British and French – known as the Allies – had more soldiers and tanks than the Germans, they were overwhelmed by their Blitzkrieg tactics. They retreated north towards the Channel, under constant attack from Stuka dive-bombers. On 20 May, the Germans reached the coast, before the Allies got there. In a surprise move, Hitler ordered the German advance to halt for three days. This allowed the British to rescue 338,226 soldiers from the beaches of Dunkirk, though they left all their tanks and artillery behind. Hitler may have believed that sparing the troops would encourage the British government, now led by Winston Churchill, to make peace.

ABOVE: British, French and Belgian soldiers are evacuated from Dunkirk. All kinds of sea-going craft were used in the operation, which lasted nine days.

FRENCH SURRENDER

On 10 June, the Italian dictator Mussolini, also declared war on France, and invaded from the south. Meanwhile, the German army was advancing south-west towards the French capital, Paris, which it occupied on 14 June. Three days later, French leaders called for an end to the fighting. Adolf Hitler felt that he had finally wiped out the shame of the German defeat in the First World War. After visiting Paris on 23 June, he said, "That was the greatest and finest moment of my life."

RIGHT: Though the French had anti-tank mines, they had not placed them in the Ardennes, where the German army broke through.

ABOVE: On 23 June, Hitler had a sightseeing trip to Paris, the city he had conquered.

HOW TO MAKE A PARACHUTE

You can make your own simple parachute using basic household items:

STEP 1
Cut out a square of about 30 cm wide from a dustbin bag.

STEP 2
Make four holes an equal distance apart around the edges of a plastic cup. Make a hole in each corner of your dustbin liner.

STEP 3
Cut four pieces of string, each about 40 cm in length.

STEP 4
Tie one end of one of the strings to a hole in the cup and the other end to a hole in the dustbin bag. Repeat three times.

Now add a plastic soldier to the cup and try it out!

STRING

FOUR HOLES IN DUSTBIN LINER

FOUR HOLES IN CUP

BATTLE OF BRITAIN

ABOVE: A badge worn by one of 88 Czech pilots who joined the RAF, and fought in the battle.

Throughout the hot summer of 1940, Allied Spitfire and Hurricane fighter planes fought a desperate battle against the Luftwaffe in the skies over Southern England. The campaign became known as the Battle of Britain.

After the Dunkirk disaster, Hitler expected Britain to make peace. But Prime Minister Winston Churchill's determination to fight on forced Hitler to plan a seaborne invasion, called Operation Sealion. At ports in France and Belgium, the Germans began to assemble thousands of barges to carry their troops and tanks. For an invasion to succeed, the Germans needed to control the air over the English Channel. Hermann Göring, the Luftwaffe chief, promised Hitler that he would sweep the Royal Air Force (RAF) from the skies. From 10 July 1940, he sent large formations of bomber and fighter planes to attack the RAF.

CHURCHILL

Throughout the 1930s, Winston Churchill (1874–1965) was a leading opponent of appeasement, warning of the dangers posed by Hitler. Proven right by the outbreak of the war, he was chosen to lead an all-party government in May 1940. As Prime Minister, Churchill strengthened British determination to resist Hitler with stirring speeches to the British nation.

BELOW: Shoulder badges worn by fighter pilots from Commonwealth countries.

NEW ZEALAND

CANADA

RHODESIA

LEFT: RAF fighter pilots scramble for their planes. Their average age was 19.

DOG FIGHTS

Much of the fighting took the form of single combat, between German Messerschmitt Bf 109 fighter planes and Hurricanes and Spitfires. Such combats were nicknamed "dog fights". Survival depended on the flying skill, and split-second reactions, of the pilots. An expert RAF fighter pilot would attack with the sun behind him, waiting until he was close to his target before opening fire with his eight machine guns. Flying daily missions was exhausting, and by September, the RAF was close to breaking point. Yet Göring had been unable to win control of the air and, on 17 September, Hitler postponed the invasion.

SPITFIRE

In 1940, the Supermarine Spitfire was the fastest and most manoeuvrable fighter plane. It could reach 590 km/h (367 mph) compared to the 550 km/h (342 mph) of the Messerschmitt Bf 109 and the 539 km/h (335 mph) of the Hurricane. One drawback was that its large fuel supply meant that, if it was hit, it was likely to burst into flames.

RADAR

Britain's secret weapon in the summer of 1940 was "radio-location", later called radar. This was based on a chain of coastal stations that transmitted radio waves to detect enemy planes. Although Göring knew that the British had these stations, he did not realise just how effective they were and made little attempt to destroy them. Thanks to radar, the RAF knew in advance where the German bomber and fighter planes were heading before they even reached the coast of Britain.

THE BLITZ

BELOW: A wrecked bus in the ruins of the city of Coventry, following a massive raid in November 1940.

In September 1940, the Luftwaffe gave up fighting the RAF in the daytime and began to bomb London and other British cities by night. The new campaign, called "the Blitz", lasted eight months and resulted in the deaths of 43,000 civilians.

The Blitz was started by Hitler as vengeance for a series of British air raids on the German capital Berlin. By hitting cities, Hitler hoped to destroy the will of Britain to fight on. Another motive was to hit arms factories, which were based in the cities. The campaign began on 7 September, when 247 German bombers attacked London's East End in relay, setting the docks on fire. "Black Saturday", as the raid was called, was just the first of 57 successive night raids on London.

LEFT: A Heinkel 111 bomber plane, flying over London. Marked by a U-shaped bend in the River Thames, the East End was easy to spot from the air.

EWK 240

> **"Everything I have has gone. Not that I mind. I'm alive and that's all that matters."**
>
> A 35-year-old East End woman, 19 September, 1940

SHELTERING

The British government built street shelters, made of brick and concrete, which could hold up to 50 people. In London, however, many East Enders felt safer in underground train stations. They brought bedding and camped on the platforms and beside the rails. At first, the authorities tried to discourage this, afraid that people would start to live underground. Yet they gave in, and some tube stations were actually closed to trains and converted into shelters.

ABOVE: Aldwych tube station in London, used as a shelter from bombs in October 1940.

COVENTRY

From November 1940, the Luftwaffe began to bomb cities in the industrial Midlands. On 14 November, Coventry, with its 21 aircraft and tank factories, was hit by the biggest raid of the whole Blitz. During a ten-hour raid, 515 bombers dropped hundreds of tonnes of bombs on the city. As fire swept through Coventry, more than 60,000 buildings were destroyed. Around 600 people died and many more were seriously injured. Despite the terrible destruction, the factories of Coventry were rebuilt, and war production was back to normal within six weeks.

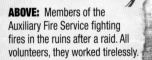

ABOVE: Members of the Auxiliary Fire Service fighting fires in the ruins after a raid. All volunteers, they worked tirelessly.

ANDERSON SHELTER

More than two million British homes had an Anderson Shelter, first issued by the government in February 1939. Made of corrugated steel panels, it was half-buried in a garden, and then covered with soil. Without drainage, it often flooded with rain water.

RIGHT: Neighbours put up Anderson shelters in their back gardens.

OPERATION BARBAROSSA

STALIN

Joseph Stalin (1878–1953) was leader of the Soviet Union, becoming dictator in 1929. Under Stalin, the Soviet Union became a strong industrial nation. A ruthless and distrustful man, Stalin held power through terror. He ran the country as if it were at war, mobilizing the whole nation in building new industries, and demanding endless sacrifices from Soviet workers. In August 1939, Stalin and Hitler made a pact, promising not to go to war with each other. Stalin believed, mistakenly, that Hitler would keep his word.

In June 1941, with Britain still unbeaten, Hitler widened the war, and attacked the Soviet Union. The invasion, named Operation Barbarossa, was to be a new Blitzkrieg. Hitler expected to conquer the Soviet Union within weeks.

Hitler's long-term aim had always been to seize "living space" for the German people in Eastern Europe. He also believed that the Soviet Red Army would be easy to defeat. The invasion, launched on 22 June 1941, came as a complete surprise to the Soviets. The Germans advanced rapidly towards the important industrial city of Leningrad, in the north, and Moscow, the capital, further south. By September, they had captured 700,000 Soviet prisoners, and Leningrad was besieged. Yet although the Red Army suffered major defeats, it was continually reinforced. The Soviet Union, with its centrally controlled economy, was suited to fighting a war. Soviet tank and plane factories were moved east, well out of range of German bombers.

BELOW: A Russian infantry cap badge.

BELOW: German tanks and armoured vehicles crossing the vast plains of the Soviet Union, in July 1941.

INVASION OF SOVIET UNION
June 1941

SWEDEN

Leningrad

Baltic Sea

Riga

Moscow

Berlin

Minsk

Smolensk

GERMAN REICH

SOVIET UNION

Tambov

Prague

UKRAINE

Kursk

River Don

River Volga

Vienna

Lvov

Kiev

SLOVAKIA

River Dnieper

Stalingrad

HUNGARY

Odessa

Rostov-on-Don

ROMANIA

YUGOSLAVIA

LEFT: Russian women dig defences in the Soviet city of Leningrad, in October 1941.

LENINGRAD AND MOSCOW

The Germans reached Leningrad in September, beginning a siege that would last almost 900 days, and end in the deaths of over one million Soviet citizens. Further south, the advance on Moscow was slowed by heavy autumn rains, which turned primitive Russian roads into flowing mud. Then, in early October, when the Germans were within striking distance of the capital, a bitter Russian winter set in. With frozen fuel, the tanks could no longer move. Expecting a short campaign, the Germans had not prepared for winter fighting. The soldiers were still wearing summer uniforms, which they stuffed with newspapers in an attempt to keep warm.

LEFT: Two Nazis try to clear a path for their car stuck in the thick mud on a Russian road during heavy rains.

BELOW: A German soldier looking weather-beaten in the Russian winter.

SOVIET COUNTER-ATTACK

Meanwhile, Stalin had been reinforcing the army in Moscow with fresh troops, from Siberia, who were trained to fight in winter. In December, the Red Army was strong enough to launch its own counter-attack. This caused a crisis in the German leadership. When Hitler's generals asked him for permission to retreat, he refused, saying, "Is it any less cold fifty miles back?" Losing faith in the senior generals, Hitler now made himself direct commander-in-chief of the army. Despite huge losses, the Germans managed to beat back the Soviet attacks, and hold on to their defensive positions throughout the winter.

RUSSIAN WINTER SURVIVAL

The war in the Soviet Union was sometimes fought in temperatures colder than -35°C. Survival in these conditions depends on:

- Adequate warm clothing

- Enough food – extra calories keep you warm

- Shelter from chilling winds and blizzards

- Proper medical treatment for conditions such as frostbite

20°C

0°C

-20°C

-40°C

BATTLE OF THE ATLANTIC

1939–1945

BELOW: Allied merchant ships in a convoy sailing across the North Atlantic.

From bases on the French Atlantic coast, German submarines, called U-boats, began a deadly campaign against British and other Allied merchant ships. All of Britain's oil, and half its food, came from overseas. Many of Britain's supplies came from the United States, across the Atlantic.

For protection, merchant ships sailed in great convoys, made up of up to 60 vessels, sailing in a dozen or more columns. On the outsides, fast naval warships, called destroyers and corvettes, hunted for the U-boats. They used sonar – sound waves that bounced back when they hit a submarine. Once they found a U-boat, they dropped depth charges. These bombs, which exploded underwater, could sink a U-boat, or disable it, forcing it to the surface.

RIGHT: The crew of a United States naval vessel watch as the depth charge they have dropped explodes underwater.

> **"The only thing that really frightened me during the war was the U-boat peril."**
>
> Winston Churchill, *The Second World War, Volume II*

WOLF PACKS

From October 1940, U-boats attacked the convoys in large groups, called "wolf packs". They waited until night, when they could surface without being seen. On the surface, U-boats were faster than underwater, and could quickly manoeuvre into position for an attack with torpedos or deck guns. A wolf pack might follow a convoy for several nights, making repeated attacks with torpedos. Every sailor dreaded nightfall, wondering if his ship would survive until dawn. Throughout the Battle of the Atlantic, the U-boats were able to sink 2,603 merchant ships. Over 30,000 British and Allied seamen lost their lives in the cold grey sea.

U-BOAT SET-BACKS

The Allies found new ways to fight the wolf packs. They developed long-range bomber planes, and a radio detection system to track U-boats by their broadcasts. In the spring of 1943, so many U-boats were sunk that the wolf-pack tactics had to be abandoned. They had suffered worse casualty rates than any other service: out of 40,900 U-boat crewmen, 28,000 died in their submarines.

LIVING CONDITIONS

A U-boat was cramped, hot and stuffy, with a constant smell of engine oil. The crew, of around 50 men, shared a single toilet. To save water, they gave up washing and shaving. The men lived on tinned food that, according to one commander, "tasted of U-boat; that is, diesel oil with a flavour of mould." Yet the crew had a strong sense of comradeship, united by the dangers they shared.

ABOVE: Using his periscope, the U-boat captain scans the surface for ships to attack.

RIGHT: In the cramped forward compartment, the crew took turns sleeping in the few bunks.

INSIDE A U-BOAT

PERISCOPE

SNORKEL

ANTI-AIRCRAFT GUN

DECK GUN

CONNING TOWER

OFFICERS' QUARTERS

BALLAST TANK

ELECTRICAL ENGINE

CONTROL ROOM

BALLAST TANK

TORPEDO TUBES

BATTERIES

TORPEDO STORAGE

PROPELLER

DIESEL ENGINE

CREW BUNKS

DESERT WAR

Between 1940 and 1943, a long narrow strip of the North African coast changed hands five times, as Allied and Axis tank armies fought each other across the desert sands.

For Germany and Italy – now known as the Axis powers – the purpose of the desert war was to conquer Egypt, occupied by a British and Commonwealth army. If Egypt fell, Hitler could seize the Arabian oil fields, and cut off Britain's supply route through the Suez Canal. The campaign began in the summer of 1940, when Mussolini's Italian army in Libya invaded Egypt. Although outnumbered, the British were able to defeat them, using Blitzkrieg tactics learned from the Germans. After breaking through the Italian lines, British tank columns swept 800 km (500 miles) into Libya and captured 130,000 Italian prisoners. To prevent a total defeat, in February 1941, Hitler sent General Erwin Rommel and a German tank force to Africa. Rommel's army was called the Afrika Korps.

BELOW: Rommel's men were proud to belong to the Afrika Korps. They wore this cuff title on their sleeves.

AFRIKAKORPS

THE DESERT FOX

Erwin Rommel (1891–1944), commander of the Afrika Korps, was the most famous German general of the Second World War. During his first desert offensive, in March 1941, he advanced with a force including dummy tanks, built from wood, mounted on Volkswagen cars, and ordered his men to stir up dust clouds. Convinced his army was much bigger than it was, the British retreated. Such cunning tactics won Rommel the nickname, "The Desert Fox".

BELOW: The German air force in Libya during 1941. Junkers aircraft were the backbone of Rommel's supply system to his forces.

LEFT: Afrika Korps troops fire an 88-mm gun, the standard German anti-tank and anti-aircraft weapon of the war.

BACK AND FORTH

The desert war was marked by rapid changes of fortunes. As an army advanced across the desert, it grew weaker, due to lengthening supply lines and tanks worn out by the desert sand. Meanwhile, a retreating army concentrated its forces until it was strong enough to launch its own counter-attack. Final victory depended on the ability of each side to send in reinforcements and fuel. Here, the Allies had a great advantage.

EL ALAMEIN

The greatest desert battle was fought at El Alamein, in October 1942. The Afrika Korps faced the British 8th Army, commanded by General Bernard Montgomery. Unlike the risk-taking Rommel, Montgomery was a cautious general, who would not attack unless he was certain of victory. He launched his offensive with twice as many tanks as Rommel, including 300 new US-built Sherman tanks. Rommel was decisively beaten, in the first large-scale British land victory of the war. Montgomery was then able to advance through Libya and Tunisia and there were also Allied landings in Morocco and Algeria. The Afrika Korps finally surrendered in May 1943.

NORTH AFRICA, 1942–1943

"We have a very daring and skillful opponent against us. And may I say across the havoc of war, a great general..."

Winston Churchill on Rommel, 1942

BELOW: Soldiers of the 8th Army capture a German tank.

PEARL HARBOR

On 7 December 1941, the United States Pacific Fleet, based at Pearl Harbor in the Hawaiian Islands, was hit by a surprise attack from Japanese bomber and fighter planes. With this shock event, the war was becoming a truly global conflict.

The Japanese had been building an empire in Asia since 1931, and in 1937 they invaded China. After the fall of France to Germany in 1940, Japan occupied northern French Indochina. United States President Roosevelt demanded that they give up these conquests. In July 1941, he cut off Japan's supply of oil, which was mostly imported from the United States. Faced with this threat to their plans, Japan decided to go to war with America. Since the United States was a much more powerful nation, Japan's only hope lay in a surprise attack on the US fleet in the Pacific.

EMPEROR HIROHITO

To the Japanese people, Emperor Hirohito (ruled 1926–1989) was a godlike figure, thought to be a direct descendant of the sun goddess. Belief in the divine status of their emperor made the Japanese feel superior to all other nations. Yet Hirohito did not directly rule Japan. Real power was held by the military, headed, from October 1941, by General Hideki Tojo, who claimed to rule on the emperor's behalf.

ABOVE: The battleship USS *West Virginia* in flames, after being hit by up to nine Japanese planes at Pearl Harbor.

ATTACK ON PEARL HARBOR

The Pearl Harbor attack was carefully planned, and led, by Admiral Isoroku Yamamoto. During the night of 6–7 December, he secretly took a fleet of six aircraft carriers to a position 440 km (275 miles) north of Pearl Harbor. Before sunrise, more than 350 bomber, torpedo and fighter planes took off from the carriers, flying in two waves. They reached their target undetected, finding the US fighter planes on the ground, where they destroyed 188 of them. Facing little resistance, the Japanese were able to sink or badly damage 18 ships, and kill 2,335 US servicemen. Yet the destruction could have been even worse – three US aircraft carriers, based in Pearl Harbor, were out at sea at the time of the attack.

RIGHT: The front page of the *New York Daily News* carried the shocking story of the Japanese attack.

BELOW: After USS *Shaw* was hit by three bombs, fire spread through the destroyer, causing a massive explosion when it reached the ammunition stores.

Franklin Delano Roosevelt (1882–1945), the only US president to be elected more than twice, served during four terms, from 1933 to 1945. He did all he could to stand up to Nazi and Japanese aggression, sending military aid to the Chinese fighting Japan and to Britain, France and the Soviet Union. However, he knew that most American people did not want to fight a foreign war. Everything changed with the attack on Pearl Harbor, which united the nation against the Japanese.

JAPANESE TRIUMPHS

The attack on Pearl Harbor was part of a bigger operation, whose aim was to conquer a vast Asian empire. On the same day as the raid, the Japanese invaded the Philippines, where US army and navy forces were based, and British-held Hong Kong and Malaya. They carried out a lightning attack before the Americans and British had a chance to react. Everywhere, the Japanese were victorious. On 11 December, Adolf Hitler also declared war on the United States. It was now truly a world war.

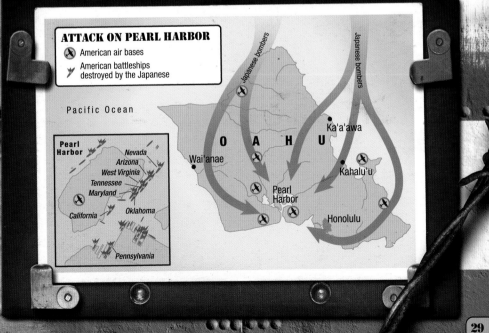

ATTACK ON PEARL HARBOR
- ✈ American air bases
- ✈ American battleships destroyed by the Japanese

Pacific Ocean

Pearl Harbor: Nevada, Arizona, West Virginia, Tennessee, Maryland, California, Oklahoma, Pennsylvania

Ka'a'awa · Wai'anae · O A H U · Kahalu'u · Pearl Harbor · Honolulu

Japanese bombers

BATTLE OF MIDWAY

BELOW: Burning oil tanks belch out smoke at Midway after the Japanese attack. In the foreground, three albatross chicks remain unharmed.

In May 1942, a vast fleet set sail from Japan for the island of Midway, in the middle of the Pacific Ocean. Admiral Yamamoto, commanding the fleet, planned to finish off the US Navy in the Pacific.

Yamamoto hoped the invasion of Midway, a US territory, would draw the US Pacific Fleet to defend the island. In particular, he wanted to sink the three American aircraft carriers that had escaped the earlier attack on Pearl Harbor. He was confident of victory because his fleet, which included eight aircraft carriers with 500 planes, was much larger than the US force. The Japanese believed that once Midway was captured they could threaten the west coast of the United States and force the Americans to make peace.

YAMAMOTO

Admiral Isoroku Yamamoto (1884–1943) was Commander of the Japanese Combined Fleet, and a brilliant mastermind who planned the attacks on Pearl Harbor and Midway. On 18 April, 1943, his plane was shot down by 16 US fighters, acting on secret intelligence. His successor, Admiral Kaga, said, "There was only one Yamamoto and no one can replace him."

"There is such a beautiful moon tonight. Shall we watch it as we sink?"

Admiral Tamon Yamaguchi, on a sinking Japanese carrier, 1942

WAITING FOR THE ATTACK

Although greatly outnumbered, the Americans, commanded by Admiral Chester Nimitz, had three advantages. The island of Midway gave their planes somewhere to land, even if the enemy sunk their carriers. Unlike the Japanese, they had radar, which would help them to find the incoming enemy fleet. Most importantly, they had broken the secret code used by the Japanese Navy to send radio messages. This meant that Nimitz knew in advance that the attack was coming. It would not be another Pearl Harbor.

SINKING THE CARRIERS

By luck, the fourth wave of US bombers reached the carriers when the Japanese planes were at low level, or on deck, refuelling. This gave them a clear run at their targets. Soon three carriers were sinking. Planes from a fourth Japanese carrier made a successful attack on the US carrier *Yorktown*, before it was also sunk by attacking US planes. With nowhere to land, the Japanese planes had to crash into the sea. By the end of the battle, the Japanese had lost 292 planes, along with their best-trained pilots. Japan had suffered a disastrous defeat.

LEFT: Two US Navy dive-bombers in action. Below the aircraft, a long column of smoke rises from a burning Japanese ship.

LEFT: Crewmen on the deck of USS *Yorktown*. The carrier is tipping over after being hit by three Japanese bombs and two torpedoes.

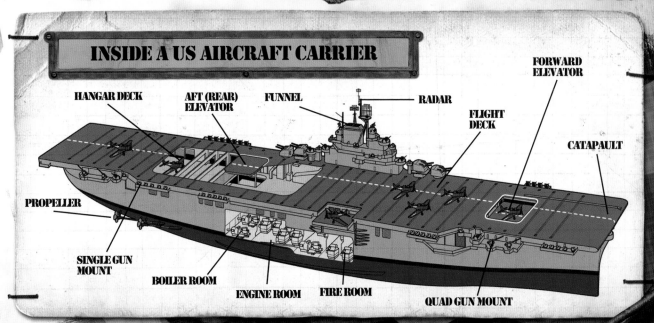

BELOW: The *Mikuma*, a Japanese heavy cruiser, in flames after being hit by US dive-bombers. Shortly after, the ship rolled over and sank.

THE BATTLE BEGINS

In the early hours of 4 June, 108 Japanese bomber planes reached Midway, where they bombed the airfields. The US fighter planes on Midway were outnumbered, and no match for the Japanese. Meanwhile, Nimitz's land-based bombers attacked the Japanese aircraft carriers, but all of them missed their targets. Then the US carrier force, positioned to the north of Midway joined the battle, sending four waves of planes to attack the Japanese carriers. The first three waves were all beaten off and it looked like the Japanese would win the battle.

INSIDE A US AIRCRAFT CARRIER

FORWARD ELEVATOR

HANGAR DECK

AFT (REAR) ELEVATOR

FUNNEL

RADAR

FLIGHT DECK

CATAPULT

PROPELLER

SINGLE GUN MOUNT

BOILER ROOM

ENGINE ROOM

FIRE ROOM

QUAD GUN MOUNT

STALINGRAD

The battle for the Soviet city of Stalingrad, which lasted from August 1942 until February 1943, saw some of the hardest fighting of the whole war. Each side saw the capture of the city as the key to victory or defeat.

In the summer of 1942, Hitler launched a new offensive. Its aim was to seize the oilfields of the Caucasus mountains, in the southern Soviet Union. If it was successful, the Germans would cut off the Red Army's oil supply, and find the fuel they desperately needed for their own tanks and planes. By August, the German 6th Army had reached the great industrial city of Stalingrad, a major port on the River Volga. The Soviet 62nd Army, which was defending the city, was less well armed than the German attacking force. But Stalin was determined that the city, which had been named after him, should be held at all costs. General Vasily Chuikov, who was appointed to defend the city, promised, "We will hold Stalingrad or die there!".

BELOW: Soviet troops defend the city of Stalingrad against German forces, in November 1942.

RIVAL GENERALS

CHUIKOV
General Vasily Chuikov (1900–1982) was commander of the Soviet 62nd Army, holding Stalingrad. He ordered his men to stay as close to the enemy as possible, seeking hand-to-hand combat. This strategy, of "holding the enemy close", meant that the German planes and artillery could not bombard the Soviet defenders without hitting their own men as well.

PAULUS
General Friedrich Paulus (1890–1957), commander of the German 6th Army, led the attack on Stalingrad. When German defeat seemed inevitable, Hitler made Paulus a Field Marshal, the highest military rank. This was to make him fight to the last man, for no German Field Marshal had surrendered before. Despite this, Paulus disobeyed orders and surrendered.

RAT WARFARE
The Germans began by bombarding Stalingrad with Stuka dive-bombers and artillery, reducing large areas to rubble. The 6th Army then fought its way into the city, where fierce street battles were fought in the ruins. The Soviets made great use of snipers – trained marksmen, who shot at the Germans from concealed positions. They travelled from one position to another using the sewers, leading the Germans to nickname the battle "*Rattenkrieg*" (Rat War). Every building was bitterly fought over. The railway station, for example, changed hands 15 times in just five days. Yet, little by little, the Germans conquered most of the city. In November, Hitler declared, "We have got it! There are only a few places not captured."

ОТСТОИМ ВОЛГУ-МАТУШКУ!

SOVIET TRAP

Unknown to Hitler, while the 6th Army was conquering the city, the Soviets were gathering large forces for a counter-attack. On 19 November, the Red Army advanced north and south of Stalingrad, encircling the Germans. Field Marshal Paulus asked Hitler for permission to break out before it was too late, but the Führer refused. The 6th Army, of over 250,000 men, was now trapped. For two months they held out, weakened by starvation and cold. On 2 February 1943, Field Marshal Paulus, with only 91,000 German survivors left, surrendered.

ABOVE LEFT: A Soviet poster shows the defenders of Stalingrad. The slogan, "Let's defend the Volga", refers to the city's river.

BELOW: Soldiers of the German 6th Army, fighting in the ruins of Stalingrad, in November 1942.

BELOW: German prisoners of war, on their way to Soviet prison camps in 1943.

"The horses have already been eaten. I would eat a cat; they say its meat is tasty."

Diary of Wilhelm Hoffmann, German soldier, 26 December 1942

KEY SNIPER SKILLS

THE BEST SNIPERS:

• choose where to fire from very carefully: a place where they can hide, but see their surroundings well.

• hide in the shade, because sunlight reflected in the telescopic sights of the rifle can reveal where they are to an enemy.

• wait patiently for just the right moment to shoot at their target.

• find another position after firing one or two shots, because the enemy will have been alerted to their position.

KHARKOV AND KURSK

The German defeat at Stalingrad was a disaster for Hitler. Yet he did not give up his dream of conquering the Soviet Union and, in 1943, two more great battles took place, at Kharkov and Kursk.

"Victory at Kursk will be a beacon for the whole world."
Adolf Hitler, 15 April 1943

On 5 February 1943, Hitler met Field Marshal Erich von Manstein, commander of his armies in the southern Soviet Union. With his confidence shaken, Hitler said, "I alone bear the responsibility for Stalingrad." It was Hitler's strategy of refusing to give up any captured territory which had led to the disaster. He allowed Manstein to use a new strategy, called mobile defence. When the Red Army attacked Kharkov, in February 1943, Manstein's forces withdrew from the front lines, giving the impression they were retreating. The Germans then waited, in concentrated pockets, for the Soviet troops to overstretch themselves. On 19 February, Manstein launched a counter-attack, around the city. By 19 March, Manstein had recaptured Kharkov, restoring the crumbling German front.

LEFT: German soldiers fire on the Soviets in Kharkov during their capture of the city.

BELOW: A Soviet T-34 tank in flames, at Kursk, during the greatest tank battle in history.

THE BATTLE OF KURSK

When Hitler's attack began on 5 July, the Soviets were waiting for it. They had been warned by spies at German headquarters. In the north, the Germans were only able to advance 16 km (10 miles) before they ground to a halt. There was better progress in the south, where the tanks advanced 40 km (25 miles), but at terrible cost. After one week of heavy fighting, Hitler, who had now lost half of his 2,700 tanks in the battle, decided to call off the attack. This brought the last German offensive in the east to an end. From now on, Hitler's armies would be on the retreat.

OPERATION CITADEL

In April 1943, Hitler ordered a new offensive, called Operation Citadel. The target was a great bulge in the Soviet front line around the city of Kursk, to the north of Kharkov. To ensure success, Hitler delayed the attack until July, when his army would have new Panther tanks, which could outclass the Soviet T-34s. This delay gave the Red Army plenty of time to prepare elaborate defences that were 320 km (200 miles) deep. By July, the Kursk bulge held 1.3 million Soviet soldiers, with 20,000 artillery guns, 3,600 tanks and 2,400 planes.

RIGHT: Soviet artillery bombard the Germans at Kharkov. The Soviets recaptured the city one month after the Battle of Kursk.

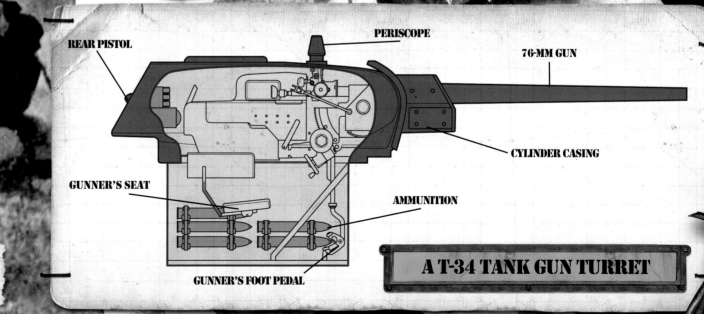

REAR PISTOL

PERISCOPE

76-MM GUN

CYLINDER CASING

GUNNER'S SEAT

AMMUNITION

GUNNER'S FOOT PEDAL

A T-34 TANK GUN TURRET

ABOVE: Soviet tanks, followed by Red Army infantrymen, attack the German forces at Kursk.

The United States and Soviet Union were the world's leading industrial nations. Unlike the Germans and the Japanese, they had plentiful supplies of raw materials, and millions of workers willing to help in the war effort.

With more than seven million people without jobs at the outbreak of war, it was easy for the United States to find workers. As more factories were built, and men joined the armed forces, the demand for labour grew. Women, teenagers and the elderly started to work in war factories. A 1942 hit song, "Rosie the Riveter", celebrated the female factory worker, "making history, working for victory".

ABOVE: B-24 Liberator bomber planes being assembled on the production line in one of the US factories.

LEFT: A US poster encouraging the war effort, showing a woman factory worker.

LEFT: To help pay for the war, the US government borrowed money from the public by selling "war bonds", a type of savings which people could later cash in.

FACTORY PRODUCTION

The United States was already a world leader in factory production. Unlike Japan and Germany, the country was out of reach of enemy planes, so production was never interrupted by bombing raids. Manufacturing methods were continually improved. In 1942, Henry Kaiser's shipyards on the west coast were able to cut the time taken to build a ship from six months to just four weeks. The United States was building ships faster than the Germans and Japanese could sink them.

AIRCRAFT PRODUCTIO

Rival aircraft companies wor together during wartime. Tho designed by Boeing, the B-17 Flying Fortress bomber was a produced in other companies factories. At their peak, these factories turned out 15 Flying Fortresses a day. In 1944, the United States produced 114,0 combat planes, more than thr times as many as the German

COMMUNIST PRODUCTION

Unlike the other wartime nations, the Soviet Union was a communist society, with no private businesses. All industries and workers were under central state control. This strong centralised government was of great help to the Soviet war effort. Soon after the German invasion, Stalin was able to have 1,523 factories dismantled, and moved east by train, beyond the Ural Mountains, where they were out of reach of German bombers. Around 25 million workers were sent to run the factories. Here, the workers were forced to work a 66-hour week. Communist rule had been widely unpopular, so Stalin presented the struggle against Germany as a "Great Patriotic War". The people were called on to defend their land against the "evil" Nazi invaders.

US CHILDREN DO THEIR BIT

In America, in 1944, up to three million children worked in factories, shops and restaurants. Younger children helped the war effort by becoming Junior Commandos. There was a military-style ranking system for Junior Commandos where promotion was earned by different acts, including:

- collecting scrap metal to recycle into guns, ships, tanks and ammunition
- picking wild milkweed pods to use in sailors' life jackets
- buying war bonds (government savings) with pocket money to raise funds for the war
- assembling care packages for soldiers at the front

ABOVE: A T-34 tank being assembled in a Soviet factory. Some tanks were painted white for winter camouflage.

SOVIET WOMEN

Communists thought that women could do the same jobs as men, including hard physical work. Women mined coal, worked on building sites and ran the railways. As they were paid less than men, they were an ideal source of cheap factory labour. By 1945, they made up 56 per cent of the workforce. About 800,000 women also joined the armed forces, as snipers, machine gunners, tank drivers and pilots. Nina Lobkovskaya, a Red Army sniper, wrote in her memoirs, "I'm proud to belong to the generation that was ready to face death for the freedom and independence of their country."

BELOW: These Soviet women are putting grease on artillery shells in a war factory.

SOVIET TANK FACTORY

Throughout the war, the Soviet factories produced 105,251 tanks, compared with 88,410, manufactured in the United States, and 67,429, in Germany. More than half of the Soviet tanks were the T-34 model. With wide tracks and a powerful engine, the T-34 was faster than the early German tanks, and had an excellent combination of mobility, firepower and armour. Even the Germans admired the T-34, which has influenced tank design ever since.

"Their T-34 tank was the finest in the world."

German Field Marshal Paul von Kleist, on the Soviet tank

HOME FRONT: AXIS

Deutsche Frauen und Mädel!

Helft mit bei der Reichsbahn!

Wenn das Arbeitsamt Euch ruft:

Meldet Euch bei den Reichsbahn-Dienststellen.

Despite their best efforts, Germany and Japan could not compete with the Allies in industrial production. They lacked fuel and raw materials, and their factories were vulnerable to bombing.

In both Germany and Japan, the government tried to control the private lives of all its citizens. Robert Ley, a senior Nazi, wrote, "The only people who still have a private life in Germany are those who are asleep." Similarly, an official Japanese publication, "The Way of the Subject", declared, "Everything is related to the concerns of the state. Even in our private lives we should be devoted to the Emperor." Every Japanese civilian was a member of a *Tonarigumi* (neighbourhood association), whose leader reported to the government on the loyalty of the members. In both countries, it was against the law to voice doubts about the war. In Germany, people who spoke out against the Nazis risked arrest by the Gestapo, the feared secret police.

LEFT: German women were not called to work in factories until 1944, but they could serve on the railways. This poster is asking women to help out.

GERMAN FACTORIES

The German economy was not completely directed to the war effort. Hitler believed that women's place was in the home, raising children, so they were not called to work in factories. War factories employed many foreign workers, from conquered lands and prisoners of war. In 1942, the failure to conquer the Soviet Union meant that Germany desperately needed more tanks and planes. Between 1942 and 1944, armaments minister, Albert Speer, tripled the production of armaments, but this would not be enough for victory.

LEFT: Heinkel bombers on the production line in a German war factory.

BELOW: Polish Jews in Warsaw are forced to clear rubble by the Germans.

RIGHT: In Japanese camps, thousands of Allied prisoners of war died of starvation, disease and beatings from guards.

SLAVE LABOUR

Both Germany and Japan used foreigners as slave labour. The Japanese forced prisoners of war to build railways and to work in mines and factories. They treated them harshly, believing that it was every soldier's duty to die rather than surrender. The Germans also had the slave labour of the Jews, and other foreign workers, rounded up all over occupied Europe and sent to ghettos and concentration camps.

HITLER YOUTH

NAZI YOUTH GROUP

German boys were expected to be members of the Hitler Youth, the Nazi youth organization. On joining, at the age of ten, they had to say, "I swear to devote all my energies to the saviour of our country, Adolf Hitler." They were toughened up with countryside hikes and, as they marched, they sang songs praising the Nazis. There was also a girls' organization, whose members were taught to be good wives and mothers.

RIGHT: Boys of the Hitler Youth parade in an open air camp, near Berlin.

晴 展   朝倉攝靈伯華

HOME FRONT IN JAPAN

In Japan's factories, old people, women and teenagers worked long hours, often seven days a week, to help in the war effort. The government told them that Japan was fighting a just war, started by the Americans. Radios and newspapers never mentioned Japanese defeats. However, life grew increasingly difficult, as food ran short, and cities began to be hit by US bomber planes.

LEFT: This postcard, showing Japanese women working in the fields, was a reminder of home, carried by a Japanese soldier.

THE HOLOCAUST

Between 1939 and 1945, at least six million Jews died at the hands of the Nazis. This deliberate attempt to wipe out the Jewish race in Europe is called the Holocaust.

Hitler had always hated Jews, blaming them, without reason, for most of Germany's problems. After taking power, he passed laws depriving Jewish people of their rights. In 1935, they were stripped of German citizenship, and forbidden to marry "Aryans" – the name the Nazis gave to members of the Germanic race. With the arrival of war, millions of European Jews found themselves living in German-occupied territory. In Nazi-occupied Poland, the Jews were forced to live in separate areas of cities, called ghettos. From December 1939, they were also ordered to wear armbands or badges sewn onto their clothing to mark them out from non-Jews.

LEFT: German soldiers round up Jewish families, following an uprising in the Warsaw Ghetto, Poland, in April and May 1943.

LOW: Jews from Hungary [arr]ive at the Auschwitz-Birkenau [de]ath camp in May 1944.

> **"Each Jew is a sworn enemy of the German people."**
>
> Joseph Goebbels, Nazi propaganda minister, November 1941

RIGHT: Auschwitz was the largest of all the concentration camps. Outside, on the train tracks, you can make out people's discarded personal belongings.

CONCENTRATION CAMPS

After coming to power, the Nazis set up concentration camps in Germany, including Dachau and Buchenwald, where political opponents were locked up. During wartime, many Jews were sent to these camps and forced to work as slaves. Unlike the German camps, those in Nazi-occupied Poland, such as Auschwitz, were built as death camps, with gas chambers. On arrival, most of the Jews were sent straight to the gas chambers, believing that they were showers. Only the strongest people were allowed to live, as long as they helped in the killing process. They were made to carry the bodies from the gas chambers to ovens, where the corpses were burned.

RIGHT: Two cans of Zyklon B, the poisonous gas used to kill Jews in the death camps.

FINAL SOLUTION

After the invasion of the Soviet Union, in June 1941, the Germans introduced a new policy of killing all the Jews they came across. Special units called *Einsatzgruppen* (special operations units) hunted down Jews and shot them. By December, they had killed 500,000 people. The following January, the Nazis drew up a "final solution to the Jewish problem". All over Europe, Jews would be rounded up and sent to death camps instead, where they would be killed with poisonous gas. To the Nazis, this was more efficient than shooting them.

HIDING FROM THE NAZIS

ANNE FRANK

Anne Frank (1929–1945) was a German girl whose Jewish family fled to the Netherlands in 1933, to escape Nazi rule. In 1942, the Franks went into hiding in secret rooms in an Amsterdam house. They remained hidden for two years, until they were caught. During this time, Anne kept a diary, published in 1947 by her father, the only family member to survive. She wrote, "I believe, in spite of everything, that people are truly good at heart."

ABOVE: Anne Frank photographed in May 1942, two months before her family went into hiding.

SECRET WAR

A great part of the Second World War took place in secret. This was the deadly world of resistance fighters and spies, who carried out dangerous operations behind enemy lines.

There was organized resistance to the Germans in all the territories they occupied. In France, resistance fighters distributed anti-German leaflets, helped escaping prisoners of war, and carried out acts of sabotage. This was dangerous work because those captured by the Germans were tortured to reveal the identity of their comrades, then shot. In 1944, the Allies, planning to invade Europe, were helped greatly by the French Resistance, who passed on information about German troop movements. Between April and May 1944, resistance fighters blew up 1,800 railway engines used by the Germans to transport troops and equipment. After the Allied invasion in June, the French Resistance fought the Germans as a proper army called the FFI (French Forces of the Interior). By October 1944, the FFI had 400,000 soldiers.

LEFT: A resistance fighter, wearing an identification armband, fights alongside Allied troops, on the way to Paris in 1944.

BELOW: Members of the FFI, in uniform, lead away a captur German solider.

LEFT: Three Soviet women partisans, in civilian clothes. They are armed with rifles fitted with bayonets.

PARTISANS

Civilians who attack an enemy in occupied territory are called partisans. In Italy and the German-occupied areas of the Soviet Union, partisans took to the mountains and forests, where they planned ambushes, raids and acts of sabotage. Many partisans were Jews, who welcomed the chance to fight the Nazis. Women played an important role in both partisan movements. In Italy, they carried messages and supplies. In the Soviet Union, women fought alongside the men. Soviet sources claim that by 1943 there were 500,000 partisans fighting behind enemy lines in the Soviet Union.

DUMMY TANKS

Both sides used dummy tanks to fool the enemy about the true size and location of their forces. Before the 1944 Allied invasion of Normandy, thousands of dummy tanks were built on the coast of Kent, in south-east England. The plan was to trick the Germans into thinking the invasion would take place in Calais, France. It was a great success. The Germans were convinced and they kept their strongest forces in the Calais area.

SPY KIT

Resistance fighters and spies needed small, specialist equipment that was easy to conceal. Here is a selection of tools carried by secret fighters during the war.

1 radio transceiver (unit to send and receive messages)
2 transmitter
3 silent pistol
4 aerial for transceiver
5 wrist dagger
6 headphones
7 receiver
8 German igniters for booby traps
9 British igniter for booby traps
10 camera to shoot documents
11 adaptor
12 power pack

RICHARD SORGE

The most famous wartime spy was Richard Sorge (1895–1944), a Soviet spy who was half German and half Russian. From 1933, Sorge lived in Japan, working as a journalist for a German newspaper, pretending to be a German Nazi. Sorge passed on many valuable secrets to the Soviet government, but he was eventually caught and hanged.

ABOVE: Sorge's Japanese identity card described him as a journalist for the *Frankfurter Zeitung*, a German newspaper.

ENIGMA MACHINE

The German armed forces sent secret coded messages created with an Enigma machine. Unknown to them, British intelligence officers at Bletchley Park in England managed to break the Enigma code and decipher these messages, greatly helping the Allied war effort. This fact was such a closely guarded secret that it was only revealed in 1974, 29 years after the war ended.

NEW TECHNOLOGIES

Victory in the Second World War depended on scientists as much as it did on soldiers. On each side, scientists worked tirelessly to develop new weapons and other inventions.

As German defeats mounted, Hitler placed increasing hope for victory on new "secret weapons". In March 1945, he told army officers, "We have invisible aircraft, submarines, colossal tanks and cannon, unbelievably powerful rockets, and a bomb with a working that will astonish the whole world." One of these projects was the German Messerschmitt-262 Schwalbe (Swallow). It was the world's first jet-powered fighter plane, reaching a speed of over 800 km/h (500 mph) per hour. Unfortunately for Hitler, it was produced too late in the war to have much of an impact.

BELOW: A V1 flying bomb, nicknamed a "doodlebug" by the British.

REVENGE WEAPONS

Some of Hitler's new weapons were called *Vergeltungswaffen* (revenge weapons), because they were used to avenge the bombing of German cities. The first was the V-1 flying bomb, which was sent over southern England. At a pre-set distance, its engine cut off, and it fell to earth where it exploded. The V-2 rocket was even deadlier. It flew at more than 3,200 km/h (2,000 mph), which made it impossible to see or shoot down. Around 1,400 V-2s were fired against Britain, until the rocket launch sites were captured by the advancing Allies.

BELOW: The V-2 rocket missile, developed by Wernher von Braun, a brilliant German rocket scientist.

PROXIMITY FUZE

One of the greatest Allied inventions was the "proximity fuze" – a radio transmitter and receiver fitted into the nose of a shell. The fuze, in use from January 1943, detected a target and exploded on approaching it. For the first time, an enemy plane could be destroyed without a direct hit. The proximity fuze played a major role in the defeat of the Japanese air force in the Pacific. Although a million people were involved in the manufacture of proximity fuzes, the weapon's existence remained a closely guarded secret until after the war.

LEFT: A shell fitted with a proximity fuze. The idea was British in origin but developed in the US.

BELOW: An atomic bomb explodes in New Mexico, releasing a lethal mushroom cloud of radiated smoke.

BELOW: A wounded US marine receives an emergency blood transfusion, using dried plasma.

TOMIC BOMB

e most deadly invention of all was the mic, or nuclear, bomb. In 1938, two rman scientists discovered a way of itting the atom, which, in theory, could ease enormous amounts of energy. wever, some of the best German clear scientists were Jews who had d to the United States to escape from Nazis. Adolf Hitler had little interest in clear physics, which he referred to as ewish physics". As a result, it was the es rather than the Germans who eloped the atomic bomb, first tested at Alamos, New Mexico, in July 1945.

MEDICINE

There were several new medicines that saved the lives of millions of soldiers and civilians. In 1940, Charles Drew, a US scientist, pioneered a new way of giving blood transfusions, using dried plasma (the liquid part of blood), mixed with distilled water. Another development was penicillin, a medicine based on a type of mould that can destroy bacteria. In 1942, a team of scientists in Oxford, England, led by the Australian, Howard Florey, found a method of mass-producing the drug. Penicillin was used to treat soldiers whose wounds became infected.

BELOW: Since the Second World War, penicillin has saved the lives of millions of people around the world.

PENICILLIN
SODIUM SALT
Glaxo
200,000 UNITS
FOR INJECTION

ALLIES IN ITALY

On 10 July 1943, the Allies, based in North Africa, invaded Sicily, Italy. The invasion force, made up of US, Canadian and British soldiers met with little resistance from the Italians.

The successful Allied invasion caused a crisis in the Italian leadership. Senior Fascists, together with King Victor Emmanuel, overthrew Mussolini, placing him under arrest. A new government, headed by Marshal Pietro Badoglio, began to negotiate with the Allies, signing a peace treaty on 3 September. On the same day, the Allies landed at Salerno, in southern Italy. Hitler was furious. While Badoglio and the king fled south to join the Allies, German troops seized control of Rome and the north of the country.

ABOVE: US paratroopers jumping from their planes over Sicily, on 10 July 1943.

BATTLE AT ANZIO

The Germans, commanded by Field Marshal Albert Kesse[?] put up much tougher resistance than the Italians had. So[?] of Rome, Kesselring set up a series of strong defensive li[?] running from sea to sea, which slowed the Allied advance[?] On 22 January 1944, US forces landed at Anzio, to the no[?] of the German defence lines. This landing came as a big surprise to Kesselring, but he rushed troops into the area and a fierce battle began.

BELOW: US anti-tank gunners fighting in Anzio, a battle which lasted for more than four months.

ALLIED INVASION IN ITALY
1943–1945

RIGHT: A German anti-tank "teller mine", used in Italy. When a tank drove over it, the pressure set off an explosion.

TIGER TANK

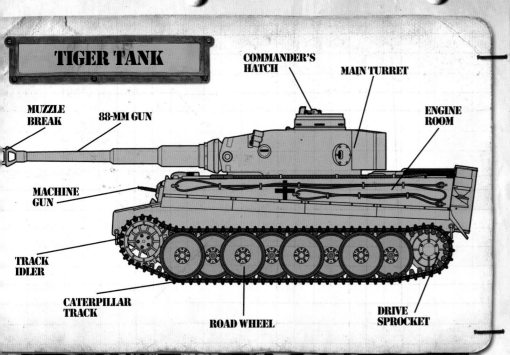

- **COMMANDER'S HATCH**
- **MAIN TURRET**
- **ENGINE ROOM**
- **MUZZLE BREAK**
- **88-MM GUN**
- **MACHINE GUN**
- **TRACK IDLER**
- **CATERPILLAR TRACK**
- **ROAD WHEEL**
- **DRIVE SPROCKET**

ABOVE: The monastery of Monte Cassino, founded in the sixth century, was destroyed by bombing, then later rebuilt.

MONTE CASSINO

With the US troops struggling to break out of Anzio, the Allies began another attack, on the town of Monte Cassino, which was part of the main German defensive line. On 15 February, an Allied bombing raid destroyed Monte Cassino's medieval hilltop monastery. The German troops moved into the rubble, where they bravely held off attacks until May. They were reinforced by armoured divisions sent by Kesselring from Anzio. On the Allied side in the battle, there were soldiers from many nationalities, including Indians, Gurkhas, Poles, New Zealanders, South Africans and French. The monastery was finally captured on 18 May by Poles, who lost 4,000 men in the assault. A few days later, the Allies in Anzio finally broke through the German defences there. The Germans were now in full retreat.

ABOVE: A crowd of Italians in Rome jubilantly celebrate their liberation by the Allies.

‸ERATION OF ROME

‸ the victories at Monte Cassino and Anzio in May 1944, the Allies swept ‸ towards Rome, which was just 53 km (33 miles) from Anzio. Kesselring, ‸ did not want Italy's ancient capital to be damaged in a battle, withdrew his ‸s from the city. On the night of 4 June, US troops entered Rome, where ‸ were given a warm welcome by the population, who hated their German ‸piers. This was not the end of the Italian campaign, for the Germans in ‸ern Italy, with their formidable Tiger tanks fought on for almost a year. ‸nd their lines, Italian resistance fighters also fought the Germans.

MUSSOLINI ESCAPES

A DARING RAID

Two months after his arrest, Mussolini was rescued by the Germans, who discovered he was being held in an Italian ski resort in the Appenine Mountains. On 12 September 1943, 90 German paratroopers, led by Otto Skorzeny, stormed the resort. Hitler made Mussolini leader of a short-lived Fascist state in northern Italy. Then, in April 1945, with defeat looming, Mussolini fled and was shot by Italian partisans.

RIGHT: Mussolini is flown to freedom by the Germans in a light aeroplane called a Fieseler Storch.

ISLAND CAMPAIGN

Following their victory over the Japanese navy at Midway, the United States were ready to go onto the attack. They began, in August 1942, by invading one of the Solomon islands, Guadalcanal, a steamy tropical island north-east of Australia.

BELOW: An American soldier keeping a look-out for Japanese in Guadalcanal in January 1943.

On 6 August 1942, 11,000 US Marines landed on the beaches at Guadalcanal, beginning six months of hard fighting. The Marines had to learn to fight in the hot and sticky jungle, where it was hard to see the enemy. The Japanese were expert jungle fighters, often attacking at night. Yet the Americans were able to bring in far more reinforcements than the Japanese, who, by January 1943, had run out of food and medicine. In February, the Japanese withdrew their last men.

BELOW: US marines landing on the beach at Guadalcanal, with the jungle directly in front of them.

ABOVE: US soldiers used deadly portable flamethrowers for the first time at Guadalcanal.

TOWARDS THE PHILIPPINES

From late 1943, the US Pacific Fleet, commanded by Admiral Chester Nimitz, advanced through the Western Pacific, capturing one island group after another. All were fiercely defended by Japanese troops, willing to fight to the last man. Meanwhile, General Douglas MacArthur, leading an Allied Australian and US army, moved up the coast of New Guinea, towards the Philippines. In October 1944, Nimitz and MacArthur came together, in a joint invasion of these islands. MacArthur, who had been commander in the Philippines when the Japanese conquered them, had made a famous promise to return there. On 20 October, he landed on the Philippine island of Leyte.

BATTLE OF LEYTE GULF

To defend the Philippines, the Japanese gathered all their available ships into one last great fleet. From 23–26 October, the rival fleets met in the largest sea battle in history, in Leyte Gulf, off the Philippines. It was an overwhelming victory for the Americans, whose bomber planes sank 24 of the best Japanese ships, including all their surviving aircraft carriers. The Japanese Navy was virtually destroyed.

ABOVE: The US aircraft carrier *Princeton* on fire in Leyte Gulf. This was one of the few American ships lost in the battle.

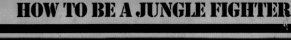

HOW TO BE A JUNGLE FIGHTER

- Move silently through the dense undergrowth. Any sound can give your location away.

- Speak as little as possible; communicate with one another by using hand signals.

- Stay alert at all times, listening hard for the sounds made by enemy troops.

- Cut down leaves to make camouflage, to wear on your clothing, to help you blend in with your surroundings.

"People of the Philippines, I have returned!"
General Douglas MacArthur, October 1944

BELOW: Douglas MacArthur wades ashore at Leyte in the Philippines, on 20 October 1944.

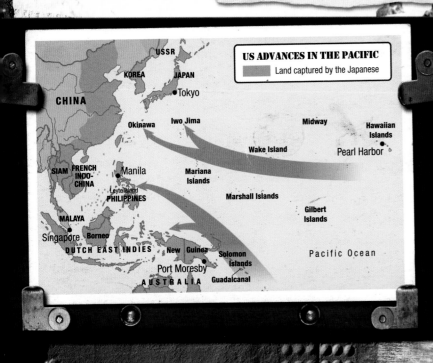

US ADVANCES IN THE PACIFIC

Land captured by the Japanese

USSR
KOREA
JAPAN
Tokyo
CHINA
Okinawa
Iwo Jima
Midway
Hawaiian Islands
Wake Island
Pearl Harbor
SIAM
FRENCH INDO-CHINA
Manila
Mariana Islands
Leyte Island
PHILIPPINES
Marshall Islands
Gilbert Islands
MALAYA
Singapore
Borneo
DUTCH EAST INDIES
New Guinea
Solomon Islands
Pacific Ocean
Port Moresby
AUSTRALIA
Guadalcanal

ASSAULT ON JAPAN

By October 1944, the Japanese government knew that the war was lost, and it was only a matter of time before Japan was invaded. Yet, the generals could not bear the shame of surrender. Instead, Japanese resistance became even more desperate.

By late 1944, the best Japanese pilots had all been shot down, and the country had little fuel left. The remaining pilots, young men with little training, had no chance of sinking ships by bombing them. So the generals asked them to volunteer to fly planes, packed with explosives, straight into the decks of the enemy ships. Almost 3,000 young men volunteered for these suicide missions. They were able to sink around 50 US ships, yet this was not enough to save Japan.

ABOVE: A Zero-Sen fighter plane, the standard model flown by kamikaze pilots

RIGHT: A young kamikaze pilot ties on his *hachimaki* headband, before flying on his doomed mission.

KAMIKAZE HEADBANDS

闘 ● 魂

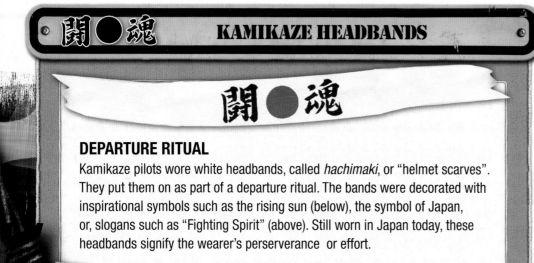

闘 ● 魂

DEPARTURE RITUAL

Kamikaze pilots wore white headbands, called *hachimaki*, or "helmet scarves". They put them on as part of a departure ritual. The bands were decorated with inspirational symbols such as the rising sun (below), the symbol of Japan, or, slogans such as "Fighting Spirit" (above). Still worn in Japan today, these headbands signify the wearer's perserverance or effort.

KAMIKAZE

Pilots who flew on suicide missions were called kamikaze ("divine winds"), in memory of great storms that had saved Japan from invasion fleets in the 13th century. Kamikaze pilots were told it was an honour to die for their emperor. On pilot, Isao Matsuo, wrote a farewell letter to his parents in which he said, "Belov parents. Please congratulate me. I have been given a splendid opportunity to di

IWO JIMA

The first territory of the Japanese homeland to be invaded was Iwo Jima, a tiny island 966 km (600 miles) south of Tokyo, where the US Marines lande in February 1945. Iwo Jima was fiercely defended by 25,000 Japanese soldiers, who had built a network of tunnels and concrete fortifications. It t over five weeks to capture the little island, and cost 6,825 American dead and more than 20,000 wounded. Almost all the Japanese defenders also d with only 1,083 taken prisoner. When their ammunition ran out, many char the enemy, armed only with bamboo spears, until they were shot down.

BELOW: Marines on Iwo Jima shelter as they blow up the entrance to a cave used by Japanese defenders.

FIRE RAIDS ON JAPAN

Meanwhile, US bomber planes were attacking the Japanese home islands. They dropped fire-bombs on Japanese cities, whose buildings, mostly wooden, quickly caught fire. By now there was almost no resistance from the Japanese air force. A huge raid took place on 9 March 1945, when 279 bombers attacked the capital Tokyo. In a great fire-storm that swept the city, between 90,000–100,000 civilians were burned to death. A survivor recalled, "I watched hundreds of people, adults and children, running for their lives, dashing madly about like rats."

LEFT: US Navy carrier-based aricraft flying over Tokyo in March 1945.

BELOW: The ruins of Tokyo, photographed from a US plane, in September 1945.

> **"The gods would weep at the bravery of my officers and men."**
>
> General Kuribayashi, Japanese commander in Iwo Jima

D-DAY

While war was raging in the Soviet Union and the Pacific, the Allies were planning the liberation of western Europe from the Nazis. A massive invasion force was being built up in Britain, in preparation for landings on the Normandy coast of France.

The planning for Operation Overlord, as the D-Day landings were officially known, began in 1943. The aim for the first 24 hours was to establish a beachhead – an area of land that could be defended against enemy attack. The Allied leaders chose American General Eisenhower as Supreme Commander of the operation, while British General Montgomery led the ground troops.

LEFT: An American soldier moves along Utah Beach on D-Day.

BELOW: This Bible – carried in an Allied soldier's breast pocket – saved its owner's life when it stopped a German bullet.

ALLIED COMMANDERS

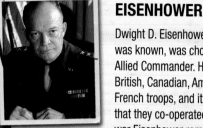

EISENHOWER

Dwight D. Eisenhower, or "Ike" as he was known, was chosen as Supreme Allied Commander. He commanded British, Canadian, American and French troops, and it was essential that they co-operated well. After the war Eisenhower remained in the army until 1952. He was elected president of the United States in 1952 and took office the following year.

MONTGOMERY

Bernard Law Montgomery was known as "Monty". In 1942, he won the crucial Battle of El Alamein in North Africa, and the following year he led the British forces in their invasions of Sicily and southern Italy.

NORMANDY LANDINGS

Montgomery planned to get around 100,000 men – plus tanks, guns and equipment – ashore in the first 24 hours of the assau Normandy was the only stretch of coastline in France which ha wide enough landing beaches. D-Day took place on 6 June 194 The assault began just after midnight as paratroops floated dov from the skies to seize bridges and road junctions. At dawn, a f of over 600 warships and 3,000 transport ships arrived off the Normandy coast. The warships opened fire on German defence Then the men began wading ashore.

RIGHT: German soldiers in a concrete bunker guard the Normandy beaches.

STORMING THE BEACHES

The Normandy coast had been divided into five landing areas. In the east was Sword Beach, where the British were landing, then came Juno Beach for the Canadians, Gold Beach for the British, Omaha Beach for the Americans and Utah Beach in the west, another American landing area. The infantry landing from special shallow-draft craft were accompanied by tanks equipped with special canvas floats so that they could "swim" ashore, ready to support the attack.

Although the fighting was savage, the landings went well in most areas. At Omaha Beach, however, the German defences were stronger than expected. The US 1st Division was pinned down on the beach by German machine-gun fire and took heavy casualties. By dusk the Americans had got off Omaha Beach, but had failed to link up with the other landing forces.

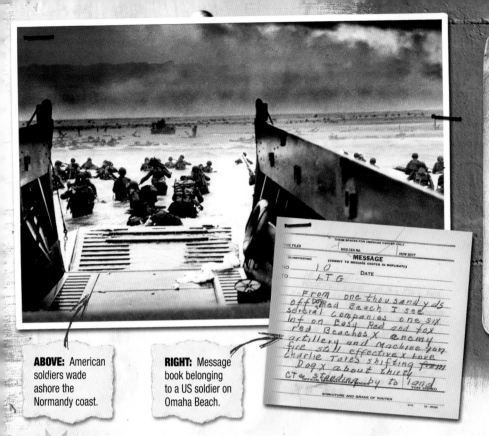

ABOVE: American soldiers wade ashore the Normandy coast.

RIGHT: Message book belonging to a US soldier on Omaha Beach.

"You are about to embark on the great crusade toward which we have striven these many months. The eyes of the world are upon you."

Eisenhower's message to Allied troops before D-Day

TANK ATTACK

By midnight on D-Day, only 132,000 men were on land, fewer than Eisenhower had wanted. The city of Caen was still in German hands – as was the town of Carentan. The Germans were bringing up reinforcements, including the 21st Panzer Division from Caen, and attacking British positions. The Allies had gained a foothold in France, but there was still much work to be done.

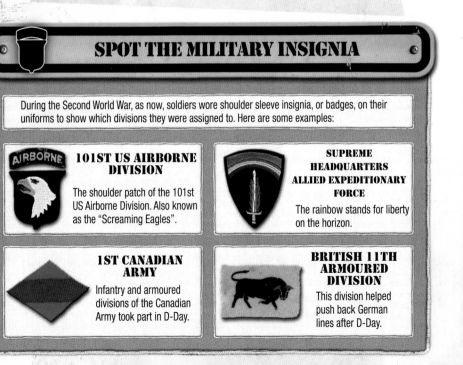

SPOT THE MILITARY INSIGNIA

During the Second World War, as now, soldiers wore shoulder sleeve insignia, or badges, on their uniforms to show which divisions they were assigned to. Here are some examples:

101ST US AIRBORNE DIVISION
The shoulder patch of the 101st US Airborne Division. Also known as the "Screaming Eagles".

SUPREME HEADQUARTERS ALLIED EXPEDITIONARY FORCE
The rainbow stands for liberty on the horizon.

1ST CANADIAN ARMY
Infantry and armoured divisions of the Canadian Army took part in D-Day.

BRITISH 11TH ARMOURED DIVISION
This division helped push back German lines after D-Day.

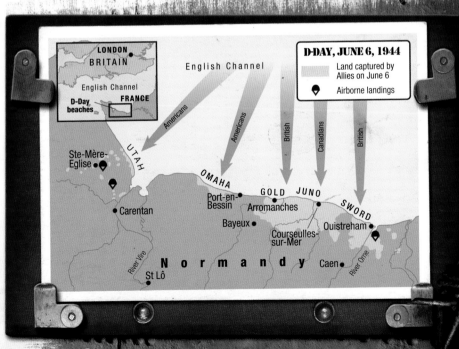

D-DAY, JUNE 6, 1944

Land captured by Allies on June 6
Airborne landings

LONDON BRITAIN
English Channel
D-Day beaches FRANCE

English Channel
Americans
Americans
British
Canadians
British

Ste-Mère-Eglise
UTAH
OMAHA
GOLD JUNO SWORD
Port-en-Bessin
Arromanches
Courseulles-sur-Mer
Ouistreham
Carentan
Bayeux
N o r m a n d y
Caen
River Vire
St Lô
River Orne

GERMAN RETREATS

Following their D-Day landings, the western Allies advanced through France, winning battle after battle. In the east, the Soviet Red Army was also advancing. Everywhere, the Germans were in retreat.

In most countries, the advancing Allies were welcomed as liberators. It was a different matter in Poland. Many Poles hated and feared the Soviets, who had invaded their country in 1920 and in 1939. There was bitter rivalry between the democratic Polish Government-in-exile, based in London, and a new government of Polish Communists, formed by Stalin in July 1944. Stalin did not want the government-in-exile to take power after the war.

WARSAW UPRISING

On 1 August 1944, the government-in-exile ordered an uprising in the capital, Warsaw, by the Polish resistance. The aim was to liberate the city before the approaching Red Army got there. The uprising lasted for two months, until it was finally crushed by the Germans. The Red Army, on the banks of the Vistula River just a few miles away, did nothing to help.

BELOW: A US Sherman tank driven by the Free French army passes the Arc de Triomphe in Paris in August 1944.

BELOW: Soldiers of the Polish Home Army, fighting from barricades in Warsaw. Around 15,000 soldiers and 200,000 civilians were killed.

LIBERATION OF PARIS

There was a much more successful uprising in Paris, staged by the French Resistance on 19 August. The 17,000 German troops in the city occupied major buildings, but did little to suppress the uprising. Hitler ordered the German governor of Paris, General von Choltitz, to destroy the capital, saying, "The city must not fall into the enemy's hand except lying in complete debris." Choltitz, horrified at the destruction of a beautiful city, disobeyed Hitler's order. On 23 August, Allied US and French troops entered the city, where the streets were filled with celebrating Parisians. Two days later, Choltitz surrendered.

BELOW: On 25 August, General Charles de Gaulle, leader of the Free French, re-entered Paris in triumph.

By 1943, many senior German army officers believed the war was lost. A group plotted to kill Hitler, overthrow the Nazi regime and make peace with the Allies. In July 1944, the plotters exploded a bomb, hidden in a briefcase, at Hitler's headquarters. Hitler survived, with minor injuries, and crushed the conspiracy. Among 4,980 people executed for being part of the plot, there were 18 generals.

LEFT: The remains of the Nazi headquarters where the bomb exploded.

LEFT: During the Battle of the Bulge, German troops in Belgium head towards Malmedy, where the Germans murdered 90 US prisoners of war.

INSIDE A SHERMAN

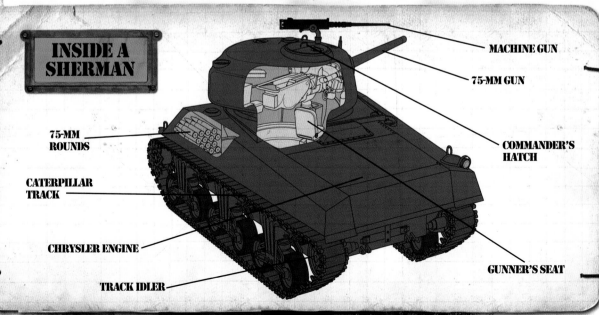

- MACHINE GUN
- 75-MM GUN
- COMMANDER'S HATCH
- 75-MM ROUNDS
- CATERPILLAR TRACK
- CHRYSLER ENGINE
- TRACK IDLER
- GUNNER'S SEAT

BATTLE OF THE BULGE

In December 1944, Hitler ordered a last, desperate, offensive, in the Ardennes. To gather enough troops, old men and teenage boys were mobilized. The attack, on 16 December, came as a complete surprise to the Allies, and the Germans managed to make an initial break-through. Yet the Battle of the Bulge was doomed to fail, through lack of fuel and ammunition. By the end, on 25 January, there were 75,000 US and 100,000 German casualties. When the Soviets began their next eastern offensive, in January 1945, the German army had no reserves left to resist with.

GERMANY DEFEATED

By the beginning of 1945, Allied armies were on the eastern and western borders of Germany, ready to invade. One key target was the capital, Berlin, where Hitler had his headquarters.

In January 1945, the Red Army began a new offensive in the east. The German forces, short of fuel and ammunition, were easily defeated. Millions of civilians fled towards the west, terrified the Soviets would take revenge for the German invasion of the Soviet Union. By the end of January, the Red Army had reached the River Oder, just 100 km (60 miles) from Berlin. For the final assault, Stalin gathered an overwhelming force of 2.5 million soldiers, 7,500 air-craft, 41,600 artillery guns and 6,200 tanks. He wanted to seize Berlin before the Western Allies got there, to impose Soviet power on as much of Germany as possible. The Supreme Allied Commander, General Eisenhower, decided to to leave the German capital to the Soviets. He knew the battle for Berlin would cost many lives and, unlike Stalin, he wanted to avoid unnecessary casualties.

ABOVE: By March 1945, the German city of Cologne, bombed 462 times by the Allies, lay in ruins. Despite 14 hits, the cathedral still stood.

BELOW: On 2 May, Meliton Kantaria, a Soviet solder, raised the red flag on the Reichstag, the German Parliament building in Berlin.

LEFT: Soviet artillery and tanks pound buildings in Berlin as they advance into the city.

ALLIED ADVANCE ON GERMANY
May 1945

BELOW: A room in the *Führerbunker* ("leader's shelter") photographed by the Soviets after 2 May 1945, when they captured it from the Germans.

IN THE *FÜHRERBUNKER*

On 16 January, Adolf Hitler moved into an underground bunker, in Berlin, where he spent the last three months of his life. From there, he continued to issue orders for German counter-attacks, which had no chance of taking place. He also told Albert Speer, head of armaments production, to destroy all the country's factories, and water and power works, to stop them from falling into enemy hands. Speer protested that this would make life impossible for the German people. Hitler replied, "If the war is lost, the German people will also perish." On 30 April, as the Red Army fought towards his bunker, Hitler shot himself. By the 8th May, the war in Europe was over.

LEFT: On April 25, 1945, advancing Soviet and US troops met for the first time at the River Elbe in Germany, and shook hands.

> **"I choose to die rather than bear the shame of overthrow or surrender."**
>
> Adolf Hitler, Last Will, April 29 1945

EFENDING BERLIN

[fro]m late April, the Red Army fought its way into Berlin from all directions. [Th]e city was defended by 90,000 German soldiers. Half of them were old [me]n and teenagers belonging to the *Volkssturm* ("People's Storm"), [th]e German home guard formed in September 1944. Although they were [gre]atly outnumbered, the ruins of Berlin gave them many places to set [up] strong defensive positions. Armed with hand-held anti-tank weapons [cal]led *Panzerfäuste* ("tank fists"), which fired high explosives from a small [tub]e, the Germans managed to destroy 2,000 Soviet tanks. By the end [of t]he battle, an estimated 70,000 Soviet soldiers had been killed in the [fier]ce street fighting. More than twice as many Germans died.

CHILDREN OF THE NAZI REGIME

BOY SOLDIERS

Members of the Hitler Youth also fought in the battle. About 5,000 defended bridges over the Havel River, on the west side of Berlin. Many were just 12 years old, and wore steel helmets too big for their heads. Within five days, 4,500 had been killed or wounded. On his 56th birthday, on 20 April 1945, Hitler made his last public appearance, awarding medals to some of these boy soldiers.

LEFT: Hitler gives Iron Cross medals to boys of the Hitler Youth in the garden of the Reich Chancellery on 20 March 1945.

ATOMIC BOMB

BELOW: A deadly mushroom cloud rises over the city of Hiroshima in Japan in 1945 as the atomic bomb is dropped.

On 12 April 1945, President Roosevelt died suddenly, and was replaced by his vice-president, Harry S. Truman. The new president was told that the United States possessed a terrible secret weapon, the atom bomb.

By now, it was clear that Japan had lost the war, yet the Japanese continued to resist. On 1 April, US troops had invaded Okinawa, to the south-west of Japan. The battle for Okinawa cost the lives of 12,613 Americans and 110,000 Japanese and Okinawans. Truman's advisers told him that an invasion of Japan itself would lead to the deaths of one million Americans. The President saw the atomic bomb as a way to end the war quickly, saving US lives.

ABOVE After taking office as president, Harry S. Truman said to reporters, "Boys, if you ever pray, pray for me now!"

LEFT: The atomic bomb was first tested at Alamogordo in New Mexico, in July 1945. Here, US workers prepare for the test.

THE ATOMIC BOMB IS DROPPED

In August 1945, the United States had just two atomic bombs. Truman decided to use them, without warning, to shock the Japanese into surrendering. The target was Hiroshima, one of the few cities not already devastated by US bombing raids. On 6 August 1945, Lieutenant Colonel Paul Tibbets flew over Hiroshima in a B-29 bomber, and dropped the first bomb, nicknamed "Little Boy". It created a huge mushroom cloud and destroyed most of the city, killing 66,000 civilians, most of whom died in the immediate aftermath of the blast.

LEFT: This bottle was melted in the intense heat of the Hiroshima blast.

LEFT: Lieutenant Colonel Paul Tibbets stands in front of his bomber plane. It was named *Enola Gay*, after his mother.

BELOW: The devastation caused by the atomic bomb at Nagasaki. This area, where houses used to stand, is two miles from where the bomb exploded.

NAGASAKI

On 9 August, the United States dropped their second bomb, nicknamed "Fat Man", on the port of Nagasaki, killing another 40,000 people. Thousands more would die later from wounds, and a new disease, called radiation sickness. For days, the Japanese leaders, who feared the Americans would depose their Emperor, argued over whether to surrender. Finally, on 14 August, Emperor Hirohito summoned them to his palace, and said, "I cannot let my subjects suffer any longer." The following day he announced Japan's surrender in the first radio broadcast ever made by a Japanese emperor. With great understatement, Hirohito declared, "The war situation has developed not necessarily to Japan's advantage." Across the nation, millions of listening Japanese people wept at the news.

END OF THE WAR

The world was very different in 1945 than it had been in 1939 when the war started. The war had created two superpowers, the United States and the Soviet Union, who would now compete to influence the world.

From 1945–51, Japan was occupied by the Allied powers, commanded by General Douglas MacArthur. With a team of legal experts, MacArthur drew up new rules of government to make Japan a US-style democracy. The people were given the right to elect their leaders, and new political parties were formed. The emperor, allowed to stay on as a figurehead, was no longer to be thought of as divine. The new rules of government declared that Japan had given up warfare forever, and would no longer have any armed forces.

LEFT: General Yoshijuro Umezu signs the Japanese surrender document, watched by General MacArthur (left) and General Sutherland.

"We, the Japanese people, desire peace for all time"

1946 Constitution, or rules of government, of Japan

VICTORY CELEBRATIONS

The winning nations all held victory celebrations. The German surrender on V-E (Victory in Europe) Day was celebrated on 8 May by the Western Allies, and the following day in the Soviet Union. In cities such as London and New York, everybody took to the streets. They danced, waved flags, and burned models of Hitler on bonfires. After the Japanese surrender in August, there were even bigger street celebrations in America. Speaking to a crowd on V-J (Victory over Japan) Day, on 15 August, President Truman said, "This is the day we have been waiting for since Pearl Harbor. This is the day when Fascism finally dies, as we always knew it would."

LEFT: Children at a London street party in July 1945, celebrating the end of the war in Europe.

RIGHT: People partying in Times Square, New York, to celebrate the end of of the war in Europe in May 1945.

GERMANY DIVIDED

After the war, the German economy lay in ruins. German cities had been reduced to rubble, and millions were homeless. The country was divided in two, with the west becoming the Federal Republic of Germany, a democratic state, allied to the United States and Britain. To the east stood the German Democratic Republic, a communist state dominated by Stalin. From 1948–51, the United States spent 1,448 million dollars, rebuilding the West German economy, to create a strong state to withstand Soviet influence. Germany now stood in the front-line of a "Cold War" between the superpowers. It would remain divided until the collapse of Communism, in 1990.

NUREMBERG TRIALS

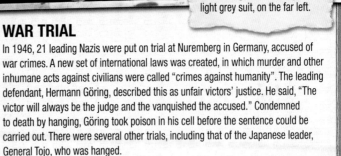

ABOVE: The Nazi defendants at Nuremberg, with Goering, in a light grey suit, on the far left.

WAR TRIAL

In 1946, 21 leading Nazis were put on trial at Nuremberg in Germany, accused of war crimes. A new set of international laws was created, in which murder and other inhumane acts against civilians were called "crimes against humanity". The leading defendant, Hermann Göring, described this as unfair victors' justice. He said, "The victor will always be the judge and the vanquished the accused." Condemned to death by hanging, Göring took poison in his cell before the sentence could be carried out. There were several other trials, including that of the Japanese leader, General Tojo, who was hanged.

ABOVE: These German children, queuing for soup in 1946, had lived most of their lives in wartime.

GLOSSARY AND INDEX

ARTILLERY: Guns used in fighting on land that fire missiles called shells.

COMMONWEALTH: Association of nations, such as Canada and Australia, that once made up the British Empire.

COMMUNISM: A system of government based on common ownership of property and industry, aimed at creating a classless society.

CONVOY: A group of merchant ships accompanied by warships for protection.

COUNTER-ATTACK: An attack by a defending force in reply to an attack by the enemy.

DEMOCRACY: Government by the people. In modern democracies, the people choose their rulers in elections.

DICTATOR: A ruler who assumes absolute power.

FASCISM: A political movement that is led by a dictator, believes that the nation is more important than the individual, and suppresses opposition through terror.

FRONT / FRONT LINE: The foremost line of an army fighting the enemy, or the scene of fighting.

GOVERNMENT-IN-EXILE: A government forced to move to a friendly country when its homeland is invaded and occupied by an enemy.

INDEPENDENCE: Freedom from control or influence.

INFANTRY: A body of soldiers trained to fight on foot.

OFFENSIVE: A term for a military campaign or attack.

RESISTANCE: A secret organization fighting the occupying enemy forces in a conquered country.

SOVIET UNION: The nations, including Russia, that formed the Union of Soviet Socialist Republics (1922–1991). Also known as the USSR.

STRATEGY: An overall plan of action for a military force.